I0088361

With Acknowledgement of the Greatest Unknown Known

Editors note: The use of lower case - i - in the first person throughout the book is a deliberate pneumonic of the author as a symbolic reminder that humility is a powerful ally in the growth and inspiration of the soul.

Book of Thoughts – Volumes I - III
Special Release   12.95 USD

109 pages

  Al Andalus Trust Media and
Miracle-A-Moment Press
A division of MMI GLOBAL, Sacramento, CA

Contact: Martin Ide, 424-202-7714
Email: alandalustrust@gmail.com

Cover Image:
"Path to Paradise: Our First Autumn" by *a'*Ali DeSousa

First Printing ISBN-13: 978-0692368961

Table of Contents

Book of Thoughts - Volume II: Divine Instance

Dedication

Many people affect and effect our lives, for the nature of humanity is that we are truly an interdependent social collective. Thus, with a loving heart and spirit this work is dedicated in the name of The Divine Sublime Supreme Lord of the Worlds with love to my beautiful children, Jabreel Dawud, Saraan Jaleh, Mekaa'el a'Ali, Imanah Mariamme, Abdul-Nuri a'Ali and a'Aliia-Sabree whose nobility of character and kindness in spirit are held in the best of hope and love in my heart.

And to my beloved a'Angela and Jordan, for the love they joyously give. Life shines with your light and promise. Also to my grandchildren Fatima, Aminah, Anissa and Donte-a'Ali with hope and promise for the generations to come.

In the spirit of joy and love my heart is humbled to posthumously offer the deepest of gratitude to precious souls who have left this measure of time. Souls held in my spirit with great fondness and adoration. Blessings and light to my father, Muhammad Abdul-Jaami, my brothers, Phillip and Ibrahim, my sisters, Donia, Lynette and Vernice. i pray your souls are within the bliss of The Infinite Existence.

i must also express my overwhelming gratefulness to my personal saints John and Clara Walker, who fostered me through the orphaned years. You did so with conviction, wisdom and love. i trust The Peace of Divine Understanding and Love is with you for all you sacrificed for so many.

Likewise to my dear family and friends who now in this life keep me on the good word and effort with genuine hearts. So with affection, i thank my sisters Mariamma, Karen, and Hana; East Coast Michael, West Coast Michael, Martin, Abdullah and Brandon; how is it that one man could be so blessed. All Praises to the Lord of the All the Universes, Dimensions and Worlds.

- STILL -

i dream in the darkness deep,
i dream in the light brightest;
frozen in awe with tears,
that tear away at the fear and doubt.

Sleep deserts me an i am as
a shadow on the deserts plain
and as the single raindrop,
in the oceans storm.

In these places where i so often abide this
mortality leave me; here...

i dream beyound the pale of mortal failing; in
The Face of The Ever Living Existence, i am
still."

<<< Illustration, Previous page
"Shadow Blossom "
© 2015 a'Ali DeSousa

Book of Thoughts

Volume I ~ **Angels Whisper**

This is one man's powerful reflections on the passages and challenges of life; a deep introspective look at humanity in the 21st century. Reminiscent of Gibran and Rumi, sage and ancient wisdom is put forth with profound clarity through beautiful prose and imagery. a'Ali DeSousa sails on a stream of consciousness that speaks to our hearts, emboldens our spirits and challenges our ideals.

In these pages one will indeed find a truth to uplift their life in an extraordinary way. Book of Thoughts speaks to the best of our nature now and tomorrow. One cannot read it without changing for the better.

- The Publisher -

Angels far from heaven lament. For it is difficult to connect, living between two universes. Sometimes a word quiets lost angels' hearts; their solitary existence surreal; angels adrift...enlightened...unaware of their dismay. With unseen wings they bleed oceans of tears, in silence; with the bidding of heaven - passed by on earth. Strangers often sought and unwelcomed...their destiny unfolds...releasing the angst of circumstance to the knowingness; that the Universe unfolds as it should.

Each day one's life is touched by angels; their wings folded from view. i hear their precious whispers in the eyes of the passerby, the plea of the indigent and the recesses of thoughts that abound.

Beyond Human

1. *The day to day living can consume your time, distract your mind and oppress your spirit. Give it pause. Remember whom and what is important. When hearts speak, angels sing, and in that moment heaven is where you are.*

2. *The mind races with the occupation of life; it embraces fear from all its own selfish demands. A mind so full with the preoccupation of work, learning, doing this and that drowns the heart's voice in its constant chatter.*

3. *The presumption of privilege and entitlement is the result of erroneous notions of social construct within our minds. We are simply one human family, one race of people no matter how many clever ways we seek to divide ourselves. It is these divisions that smother our hearts.*

4. *War begets war and nature is an unmerciful foe. Our planet is at risk from mankind's ignorance and neglect.*

5. *A good intention practiced is a kind act; a kind act repeated, is a goodly behavior; a good behavior repeated, is a wonderful habit; a wonderful habit repeated builds beautiful character.*

6. *In such beauty the storms of oppression and strife are quelled.*

7. *One cannot complain of this world's misery and unkindness, when one has let the sun set without a kind deed to another.*

8. *Shall i tell you of a great thing that even in silence changes all who see it? Shall i tell you of a small thing that connects the most disparate people? If i tell you this thing's value cannot be quantified by any measure of the market, yet it*

is the most valuable asset one can own, would you believe me?

9. Well i know this all to be true...just smile at the world from your eyes, from your mouth and from your thoughts. This is a most valuable thing. Tell me now if i have erred.

10. Tradition is the imprint of those who live and love before you. Live and love strongly, do good endlessly without concern of reward. Your imprint may too become a tradition.

11. Tradition itself is an evolving thing.

12. Awake with thankfulness, many souls will not find the sun this day.

13. Each breath drawn is from the Core of Existence itself. Each breath drawn is from the Primordial Source of The Infinite. We are

vessels of the breath…life; oh, humanity each vessel is sacred.

14. *At the core of all oppression is greed. It does not matter what the greed is for. Lust for power, wealth and or control are all the same; greed. The most heinous form of greed is the social construct of privilege of one social group over another.*

15. *As long as any social construct at any time predicates its existence in a claim of privilege over another social group, then the seeds of discord are sown. And surely take root in myriad 'isms.'*

16. *These flawed intellectual concepts mask the disease of the heart and soul.*

17. *Humanity's ever evolving experience seeks to express the poetry of life; through invention, music, art and words. Yet, the sum total of knowledge now and in the future will never truly express GOD.*

18. *Bliss exists not only in our giving; but accordingly in our receiving. Be ever grateful for the generosity of love's giving and receiving, it is of The Divine.*

19. *The world and its' events will oppress one's faith, but for those who sip from the fountain of belief persevere through their trials. Knowing that ease is assured for the believers. The believers kindness and radiance outshines the stars of the heavens.*

20. *GOD's bounties will not circumvent the believer. GOD is as we believe and so it has been written.*

21. *This is the promise of The Most High; then the angels' whispers echoed 'less we forget, less we forget, we.*

22. *Let us be true to what we profess to believe, release what is not meant for us with grace. Letting kindness reek from our beings, loving with sincerity and honor; this is living with elegance.*

23. *And know that such living will always be greater than all our gathering up.*

24. *Oh mankind, cry from the heart, The Beautiful and Perfect Attributes, these are the vibrations of unseen resonance of creation itself. Chords of The Splendid that open the heart and attune you to love one another in truth and not despise each other.*

25. *Certainly, this is nearness to The One, Infinite Love and Beauty.*

26. *Cry these names in earnest no matter your liturgy, for in fact they remain from before time and you shall be inclined towards one another*

Regarding Women

1. *Her spirit smiled the first time he glanced her way; he seemed to notice far more than her physical grace. He tendered words with warm resonance. The fragrance of his virile musk scent, soft-strong hands that made her flesh sing.*

2. *Now, like iron cold steel, his hands make her head ring...her mouth agape; the taste of blood, body and soul searing with pain, meets a new day.*

3. *Now, his charm, touch and passion all a vulgar pretense...but she is silent.*

4. *i wonder why the hands of man injure her body, and his words strangle her soul.*

5. *The moon was high in the sky, the heavens felt her heavy sighs, tears from her heart rains on my sleep; in the depth of the night there is a faint a radiant light.*

6. *Silence the garment that shields her soul; there is something greater to make her whole.*

7. *Still, i wonder why the hands of man injure her body, and his words strangle her soul.*

8. *My heart whispered dear beautiful daughter we embraced this morning under a golden misty sky; an aura of love and ebullience that cannot be described.*

9. *As you leave, quiet tears i did hide...My spirit solemn wondering if your life is to be spared the violence our world too often, still denies.*

10. *So to my room i secluded myself; my hearts floodgates could not be denied. A quaking chest, trembling i stroke the keys, a blurry screen before misty eyes.*

11. *Oh Divine Protector, spare the women of this heart; let your Divine Grace be within me. Let not the anguish of their souls go unrequited.*

12. *Even the earth mother anguishes over our inhumanity to one another; she screams and cries. She is trembling; her breath and tears are cast upon us. So, the land quakes and the seas surge over us.*

13. *Peace cannot be found for the lust of what is treasured in her--the earth. Through her grief, she moans so passionately. Grieve with her...for us.*

14. *What can you say about a species that does not protect its future, our women and children?*

15. *And then trembling, the moment left my immortal being to be covered in the darkness edof yesterdays' truth.*

16. *Through the key hole he saw his mother on the floor, a hand crashing down upon her again; in that moment he learned never to complain.*

17. *i know this boy well he lives in my heart; he sees through her eyes...in many ways their pain never stops.*

18. *The scars and bruises upon her body make her cringe from her babies touch. The wounds within her mind, the thunderous trampling of her spirit is a greater pain upon her soul.*

19. *Oh Divine Protector, spare the women of this heart; let your Divine Grace be within me. Let not the anguish of their souls go unrequited.*

20. *This pain humanity cannot afford to suffer.*

21. *The violence against the mothers of humanity stains the heart of man.*

22. *She does and says things different and you like it. Her laugh lightens your heavy day. You*

can't figure it out, but it just does. You just like her the way she is. The answer to this is simple, you love her. The woman who comes into your life like this is rare and you know it. Your heart is her home. Keep it safe.

23. *For weariness and fatigue will be upon you; and then the embrace from your weary heart to the one who honors you as you honor them causes pause, and you feel their weariness and fatigue. Yet, in this suspended moment the blend of your exhaustion causes restfulness to settle on your spirits. And you both are better for it.*

24. *There is not love without honor.*

Compassion and Beauty

1. *The compassion inherent to every soul is obscured by the mind's ambition, analysis and vague ramblings. What is theology, philosophy, if not to foster what is innate to the very creation of humankind.*

2. *Compassion does more than meet the mundane needs of society. Compassion is a sublime universe within each person waiting to be born. When born through you, it beckons all with The Light of Divinity.*

3. *When one's wants for this or that dissipates, then the mind quiets. The heart's song emanates with virtue; a melody that touches all with serenity. No motive to acquire exists in that moment.*

4. *When one becomes nothing, one becomes everything. This is how one's solitariness gives birth to compassion and one's duress becomes their beacon.*

5. *For the calamity of others is never voided by the heart of the true; it lingers beneath the joy, a shadow of sorrow an unending supplication sent to heaven.*

1. *It only takes the pause of loss...and the embrace of love; to reawaken us to the sublime intangible nature of life.*

2. *Why do we let all the other emotions override love? Love is more than just an emotion. It is the quantum fabric of Existence Itself. That which you believe GOD is Light Ordered Vibrational Energy, A fathomable quality of The Infinite Ever-Living Majestic Beautiful Origin it is ever present. Why then let anger, jealousy, hate, disconnect you from The True Reality?*

3. *Then, i sat quietly for the angel's voice silenced.*

4. *Love is the attribute that emanates from the courageous.*

5. *There is knowingness within the soul beyond the cognition of the mind; a reality intuited from the heart consciousness, aligned with the resonance of The Divine. In such a moment there is truth, in such a moment this thing we call love can be found, gained and kept.*

6. *It is hope that shields the soul from the atrocity of injustice; but the shield shatters if one hopes rest in the fallible.*

7. *In the face of every calamity, there are countless possibilities; the one constant is hope. Hope is not a mindless whim; it is healing optimism pursued energetically;*

8. *Each breath is hope.*

9. *There is a thing for some so fleeting, colored by senses; but you know with me, this is not a fleeting thing. It is a thing from the eye of GOD, which causes the heart to beat. And it is this that keeps you with me.*

1. *To the people of world who perpetrate heinous acts in the names of GOD and prophets: you are liars.*

2. *Those who claim these reprehensible deeds for GOD, justice will find you for your treachery against the innocent. Know that the law of balance is immutable. Recompense will find you and no helper can then avail your soul.*

3. *Superiority, false judgment, privilege, envy and all the 'isms' are the obstacles to peace.*

4. *Why do the peacemakers spend so much on war? Why do the profit so much from the maimed suffering? Why do the so called peacemakers revel with their promises of the specter of death?*

5. *Social or religious hegemony will not establish peace.*

6. *Do you not believe the son of man who promised to whom will inherit the earth? Do you not heed the Prophet of the desert on the taking of life?*

7. *Peace is not merely the absence of violence. It is more powerful and sublime than this.*

8. *Peace is not a goal; rather it is a dynamic state of being. The message is sealed and made clear.*

Perception

1. *The appearance of things is a matter of perception; perspective is unique to each being. Ultimately one's reality is only this.*

2. *Understanding this, we are nothing, we are everything. All divisions are our illusions of perception and perspective.*

3. *Our perceptions are like the facets of a jewel, they reflect the light of our souls -- in many colors to the world.*

4. *There will be moments, days of dismay. Still, there is the joy of understanding. This makes those times precious in the unveiling of life.*

Life, Joy and Happiness

1. *It is not the headlines that tell the story of the world and life. We do not choose those moments or the magnification of them. The moments that we share with strangers, friends, and family...the quiet ones we live alone are life's radiant gems.*

2. *A moment of kindness can birth a life of hope.*

3. *Within each droplet of rain there is a universe of elements and the very force that gives life. We are but raindrops of consciousness upon the earth.*

4. *Perhaps heaven exists in what brings delight to the heart and spirit. Heaven exists within our capacity to be vessels of love and hope.*

5. *Think globally, act locally; just make a difference in life. Don't wait for wealth, or*

others. Let the acts of your own volition change the world for the better.

6. *The warnings of a generation have come to pass; Orwellian news echoes relentlessly with fear of unending war. We've forgotten our youth and exuberance when we cherished the earth.*

7. *When we warned our parents of our nation's arrogant folly in the quest global predominance...now we are parents and none the wiser, it seems.*

8. *Do not let fear cover you, though the experts blast it on screen; change is inevitable.*

9. *Nobility in leadership, justice and fairness have vacated the hearts of too many.*

10. *It is said; ...what is greater than love lost; found, gained and kept... i agree.*

11. *i heard the voice of Muhammad; i felt the touch of Jesus, and the breath of Buddha caress my face. My heart says love them so i do.*

12. *Could it be that we aspire to a thing that is for the enrichment of a few? What if we aspire to what can be enjoyed and for the benefit of many?*

13. *Seeking the face of The Infinite seems as futile as returning to the womb without faith. Sincerity in faith blossoms into belief; with belief comes knowingness.*

14. *The Unknown Reality of The Indescribable One is evident. Present in the eyes of every living thing, there is The Omnipresent Reflection of The Existence.*

15. *One only needs to see.*

16. *Resolutions often do not manifest, perhaps they were only whims. Resolve to take the journey towards your goal. Live the journey and inevitably you will surpass your resolution.*

17. *Knowledge is like the sun to a garden; if one does not bask in it, one will wither.*

18. *We can accomplish many things and be exhilarated pursuing our dreams; but to arrive at the destination alone, will find one's soul wanting.*

19. *Our world in its activity and physical manifestation goes through the upheaval at the dawn of a new age. i am reminded that life is a menagerie of coincidences...that is a sum total of experiences that perfectly coincide...a synergistic synchronicity. Every chance meeting no matter the forum or mechanism is not random...but a perfectly designed opportunity.*

20. *Each moment is an opportunity to experience, learn and to discover something new...new, within ourselves and others. We are only bound by the limits of our thoughts...yet, thoughts are infinite.*

21. *Consciously choose on which to act upon.*

22. *Dreams are fantastic illusions unless we dare to pursue them.*

23. *We can choose to live in a world not defined by the borders of nation states. We can choose to live in a world not encumbered by an antipathy of political ideals.*

24. *We can choose to live in a world beyond the religiosity of intolerance and GOD competition.*

25. *We can choose a walk that lets the heart settle in the serenity of being human. No presupposition of privilege or superiority.*

26. *It is only the flaw of human reasoning that leaves us wanting. Our desire to possess what only can be known when we are present. That is those moments in humility, when we are truly present and love abounds.*

27. *Tears are the laughter of an unburdening soul. Laughter is the cry of a soul in momentary joy.*

28. *There is a quiet joy and ebullient breath with pause; witnessing the unfolding blossom of feminine beauty; an intangible far beyond the corporeal form with all her grace.*

29. *Joy is often induced by the most random and unexpected things; be random, be the unexpected.*

30. *Happiness is a state of being that is filled with tears and smiles; layered with joy and sorrow. Happiness is a condition of the*

heart; *from which one loves, despite circumstance.*

31. *Happiness exists within the being; pleasure is often sought, when achieved happiness may have been lost.*

32. *Happiness is a decision. Happiness is not a moment achieved; rather it is a state of being. Pleasure is those sensations which pass fleetingly.*

33. *When ordinary people do a little extra; the world becomes extraordinary.*

34. *They are there for the moments you hoped, at times they are not. The sincere of them strive to be better and hope their children understand. They are fathers.*

35. *Words are more than the sum of their syllables; they stir the soul for better or*

worse. Without words life would be wanting.
For even the unspoken can be heard.

36. *Distances in space are far greater than the*
    distance of true hearts.

37. *Patience is the virtue which leads to all*
    virtues. Perhaps actions taken through
    patience will manifest our highest
    aspirations.

38. *Technology is a wonderful convenience; but*
    the most powerful and beautiful things in
    life transcend it.

39. *Profit gained without personal efforts in*
    labor is the precursor of poverty.

On Being Men

1. *How is that women and children fall victim so much to the avarice of man? How has man forgotten their essence began in his very loins?*

2. *Oh, that one considers himself a man; but the seeds of the nations churning in his loins are spilt carelessly, and without consideration. This seed, vibrant with the life force of a species, reduced to mere recreational pleasure.*

3. *How little we value the power of creation.*

4. *Oh man, will you silence your drums of war? Silence, is not the absence of sound; it is the resonance of stillness. In this quietude inspiration, vision and hope register within the heart.*

5. *So, be still for a moment. One can better see where one is going...within the eye of the storm there is calm. In this place you will discover your folly. It is here, that penitence for the misery put upon your women and children, can be gained.*

6. *A man goes off to war and lauded for his courage. War is a consequence of our corrupt hearts. It does not take courage to take a life.*

7. *Facing death may be courageous; yet death is always an eminent reality.*

8. *There is a greater courage found in living and sustaining life. Only the courageous and committed people can change the world; the only thing that has or ever will.*

9. *So let man uphold life over destruction. Let his hands bring forth the advancement of life, just as future nations churns within his loins.*

10. *And let the words of men soothe the distress of his children and comfort the heart of his beloved wife. Let not his family fear him. Then his nation will be of the just ones.*

11. *Let her not be a play thing to you. But the garment of your soul and let her be the one who receives blessings from the sanctuary of your heart.*

Heart Thought

1. *Do we only have five senses? Does not your heart have a voice?*

2. *Now is the moment we have, if it is the last may your heart be glad of it.*

3. *You cannot see in others; except that which you have seen in yourself.*

4. *Only from the winged heart of your soul can you touch heaven's door.*

5. *The beat of her heart heralds our hidden beginnings; in life the drum beat encourages joyous feet.*

6. *Life is an improvisational dance, breath by breath let the rhythm move our feet.*

7. *Friendship is a sublime chord; entwining threads of kindness, loyalty and trust. Friendship is the rope that lifts us when we*

fall and guides us back to earth when we soar.

8. Friendship is the radiant and splendid couch in which the beloved recline; and intimately their soul burst free from the confines of the corporeal.

9. Hearts that echo with The Sublime Power do so with soft smiles. These impulses give birth to hope wherever such hearts would be.

10. What can settle the heart more than the timbre of the angel's chorus? A lilting melody that caresses the soul and enlivens the spirit.

- UNSEEN -

Beneath the barrenness, awaits the bounty of life manifest.

This is the mystery of the unseen.

This is the reality of the Greatest Unknown Known.

Hidden in purest form; apparent within everything, we come to know.

Book of Thoughts

Volume II ~ **Finding GOD**

Forward

Faith is a matter of the heart and soul, though the words and vehicle of expression may differ; its truth lies in the reality of the believer. GOD is as the servant believes.

Prologue

i dream in the darkness deep, i dream in the light brightest; frozen in awe with tears, that tare away at the fear and doubt. Sleep deserts me and i am as a shadow on the deserts plain and as dryness in the oceans storm. In these places where i so often abode this mortality leaves me; here i dream beyound the pale of mortal failing in The Face of The Ever Living Existence i am still.

Tears Reign, Tears Rain

1. *Tears reign, tears rain for the anguish of souls that visit in the first hours of the morning, the unsettledness of the world its beings, overwhelms who i am, even now, in these moments of restoration. Oh mankind, why can't you see that our destiny is more than the cleverness of what we wrought from our minds and hands.*

2. *Tears rain, tears reign over this heart that can't understand the selfishness pervading our collective souls; does not anyone hear the voice of wonder and majesty.*

3. *Or are all our breaths to be consumed with hunting and gathering. This heart is stirred by the lament of angels and souls carried on the night wind.*

4. *Tears reign, tears rain, the love that people swear they hold, is so careless that and*

unkind as to injure the spirit and crush beautiful hopes and dreams.

5. Oh, mankind this wheel of self indulgence and worship casts a shadow on the true being within. i watch new stars born in the heavens, and the light of souls crushed on earth by lies of pretense not love.

6. Tears rain, Tears reign, in a world where more choose to possess and seek the gratification of their own desires; blind from The True Reality of Being.

7. Oh mankind; want what you want when you want it, and see the destruction that reeks from your very living. The lament of angels and souls carried on the night wind still stirs this heart.

Times Illusion

1. *The years fly by; but the smiling face of an old friend suspends time.*

2. *The earth, its mountains, and waters, its creatures that crawl, those that walk and fly; await for us to shine our light, that streams to and from Divinity. Fear...only makes us cowardly and our world needs its true champions.*

3. *Champions that do not hide behind ideology, religiosity or on military might yes you, who were imprinted before birth with what the world needs right now.*

4. *Thankfulness is a state of being, not a designated moment in time. Bless you always, Ya Yarweh, Ya Jehovah, Ya Jeshua, Ya Allah, Barukh!*

5. *Time is never lost, it is only a measure. It cannot bind the spirit of life's challenge.*

Measures by chronometers, watches, sundials or by celestial bodies are not of significant consequence; when placed within the infinite intuitive knowingness of the heart.

6.   *They asked: Does anything last forever; family, friends, lovers or any attachments in their various shapes and forms? Forever is a construct that can only known by the heart.*

7.   *There is only 'The Present.' As we unfold in our consciousness of spirit and soul, all things are within The Unbounded Infinite. There is just always. Yet we perceive not.*

8.   *Beauty, it is beyond any attribute of the body and more than the glowing aura of your countenance. Embraced within the word that whispers from the heart is a moment where i do not exist.*

9. *That is when the truth of love, kisses the spirit of the soul...the soul that knows yesterday and tomorrow before it dawns.*

10. *Cloaked in that moment of beauty, truth sings from this heart.*

11. *Though only an arbitrary device, it waits not in the measure of things. Stillness is not lack of motion but a state of being.*

12. *All one has is the very moment of now. Only in this does time truly exist. We are a small aspect of The Balanced Continuum.*

13. *When we inhale that is the only known that matters in the moment. What thoughts and emotions within us are reinforced and energized by that breath.*

14. *There is no guarantee that we will exhale. Life is really that simple, yet intrinsic.*

15. *Breathe well.*

"Perfect Imperfection"
by a'Ali DeSousa

1. *The power in our prayers and belief magnify, when the overwhelming of life leads us to cry to GOD, The Divine Origin. Surely, as great as is our difficulty; greater will be the relief when in sincere humility we bend prostrate fall.*

2. *The Divine Ever Living Existence is only experienced never truly defined. All religions, philosophy and prose are mere faint shadows of shadows cast by The Light within the soul.*

3. *What is the youthful lively thing surging within the breast; though it is sunken and sallow with years? Your breath is the wind of The Divine. What more is there to ask for?*

4. *Neither science nor religion can prove GOD. These are mere experiences of the mind entrapped in the concept of time.*

5. *The Great Omnipresent Omnipotent Omniscience cannot be framed in the languages of our species. The Unknown Known is perceived through nature, consciousness and more than this.*

6. *Only the heart can know The Infinite Ever Living Existence.*

7. *This soul's light embracing your being and the smile like the moon lighting the shadows; in a twinkling can fade. In a short time passing, they are empty and know you not; as the heart wretches with fear, despair and sadness.*

8. *Oh, that we guard not the beauty and trust of our souls. Crying to The Truth Beyound Comprehension is the only solace in this devastation; and so this heart weeps.*

9. *This place where the soul lives this body can become frail; this mind in which from which the soul tries to speak becomes distracted. Together this tandem chorus of the ego turns on the soul and will smother it with illusions and their tricks.*

10. *Oh, how the ruin can bring misery to lives save the ones in which the soul comes to know; that it is the Master.*

11. *It alone is a child of The Eternal. It alone is the inheritor of the Lord of Majesty and Bounty. This world many prefer to be distracted and few become servants of the Master. Oh, Beloved do you understand?*

12. *What shall bring the hearts of people together? Even the callous grieve. None is an end unto their self and indeed belief in one greater than the self has more than once brought magnanimous change to better the human condition.*

13. Our social whole is the collective out pouring of our hearts. There are hearts that find satisfaction in the confirmation within and in acknowledging The Divine Unknown Known. Still, it is this awe and wonder that inspires still great things among us.

14. Shall i tell you of something so profound and deep that all the words of all the languages are exhausted in the effort to bring its context to mind?

15. Shall i tell you of something so simple that a single word from any tongue makes it clear to those who know? Yet, it is only one thing i speak of.

16. Shall i be so bold to testify that it is the only reality of existence; and from it all came to exist? Or is it brashness, arrogance or hubris that would bring such a claim to ones voice...nay, insanity or imbecility?

17. *Yet, i tell you what every noble being, sage and saint has told you and what ones idea of religion obscures from them. Love is heaven's reality, Love is life and Love is The Divine Continuum of Creation.*

18. *GOD is Love. Few find this truth.*

19. *When slumber silences the world her voice pierces consciousness. When the mind's eye opens to The Infinite, it is GOD's indescribable visage that appears.*

20. *The sun and the moon are heaven's lanterns for the earth; and they compete not or diminish one another. Be like this one to the other and your love unfolds in peace that surpasses all understanding.*

21. *The Evident Perfection will be with you, always.*

22. *We are the reflection of unfolding Perfection, less we forget, we.*

1. *Should Mercy evade you? Shall Compassion be voided for political sentiment? Look upon the heavens and the wonders so confounding. Look how the plants, and trees provide for you with their breath, as indeed we provide for them with ours, is this not a Mercy through our own evident nature?*

2. *Thought is not necessary for this most excellent symbiosis.*

3. *Being Human is for The Evident Compassion to resonate in each breath as well. Why let the emotional tides of history continue our enmity towards one another?*

4. *What is humanity's aim in the war and suffering we wreak upon one another and the planet; yes, even now up into the heavens?*

5. *We have gained not my beloved.*

6. *The Evident Sovereign Existence is not bound by our acquisition of scientific knowledge, though in this there is a freedom of truth if one could see.*

7. *Nor is the Sovereign Ever Living bound by the limits of our expressed thoughts in any form. Do the genteel of the earth seek to contain GOD in their religion?*

8. *Such a thing is not possible.*

9. *Relinquishing our imposed identity to discover our humanity within the spirit of the heart can soothe sorrows and embolden hope.*

10. *So, i smile through tears as The Sovereign Merciful Compassion uplifts me from religiosity to The Evident Ever-living Reality; i pray by the sacred breath within the compass of my awareness.*

11. *Teach me to tread lightly in this world and to see the face of GOD through enmity; wash away my prestige and arrogance so that the lives of others can be uplifted.*

12. *Let not these souls claim anything except to gain understanding through The Mercy, The Compassion of The Sovereign Awareness; i beg from this poorest of hearts to be more human.*

13. *Oh sentient species…why do you forgo your intelligence? Why does the triviality of your emotional dysfunction consume your being?*

14. *You witness, The Pure One; Whose throne unlike any monarch is beyond our conceptualization. There reigns The Perfect Truth, this thing we call the Universe Its' shadow. A glimpse of the apparent Evident Pure Truth before us.*

15. *We see it, feel it with our senses and perceived within the sublime aspects of our nature. Our consciousness pauses in unfathomable awe when we truly observe it. Countless galaxies and celestial phenomenon are in constant birth in the perceived blackness of space.*

16. *Yet, this is only minute evidence of The Pure One from which this spectacular enormity emanates.*

17. *The Perfectly Pure One is The Source of Peace, The Balance; the place from which The Balance Origin of Peace is clear as we witness more and more of creation. The Inspirer of Faith, The Inspiration is The Immutable Constant of Change ever evolving.*

18. *Computations of our greatest mathematics humble the best of minds; to declare within the recesses of thought, GOD, The*

Unexplainable! GOD, the Great Unknown Known!

19. *Reflecting upon The Inspiration, The Inspirer of Faith raises the hair upon my limbs. This heart's ebullience is filled within the moment of The Perfect and Evidently Pure. Within this instant of grace the intellect is crushed by an unfolding understanding. The Perfect Peace,*

20. *The Source of Balance consumes my soul and i rest in momentary bliss. May this touch from The Compassionate Mercy, ever change the being i am becoming.*

21. *Oh, that a soul yearns what its' heart knows, this is to be beyond the frailties of body; becoming more than human.*

22. *Breathe now, in The Pure Inspiration The Source of Peace all is manifest through The One Manifest Inspiration; Whose aura*

brings us faith; this same power and grace is within this breath.

1. *Through the night i travel to many places not found in wakefulness. These journeys are not dictated by the volition of cognitive thought.*

2. *Though the night confines of space and time i submit to an unknown will. i laugh, smile, run, as tears reign my consciousness; and tears rain from my soul and their dampness on my skin is evident; though in truth i am far from flesh lying in a distant room.*

3. *The profundity of these experiences is ever etched in the mind. The return to this body to greet wakefulness is a miracle of life;*

4. *Thus i stand, bend and prostrate fall to The Guardian of it All.*

5. *The Victorious One, The Victor brings the triumph of the breath within this mortal shell and i go forth in this new day of discovery. The Faceless Victor's armor is*

sublime but clearly mirrored in everything i see.

6. *The Victorious One that claims this living is The Guardian of my death in slumber; and triumphs within the ever impending sleep with no breath.*

7. *Yes, this Guardian of my spirit and soul moves the oceans tides, the winds, The Guardian Victors breath. Surely, The One Whom Compels Creation's Expansion is witnessed now without end.*

8. *This mental prowess once claimed with such vanity, now a shattered idol that sets my soul free.*

9. *In wakefulness or sleep; unbound from corporeal angst; The Compeller of the Expansion, moves this living called life.*

10. *This beating thing in my breast is not the heart of what i am. This humanity releasing in my action is the faintest glimmer from The Victorious Guardian, The One Whom Compels Creation's Expansion.*

Water Sanctuary

1. *i sit under the rushing mountain falls, peering out into the forest green; the astounding beautiful plush varieties of vegetation, mountain peaks, fragrant-- pungent blooms and the wild languages of beasts arrests my being.*

2. *The dampness of the air and the subtle sprays soak my garments to a frigid transparent second skin...still am i. Immobile in a surreal majestic; yes this chaos of natural life...cleanses my soul.*

3. *The Truth of The Greatest unveiled in my desperate situation wrapped with night's curtain, under the jeweled summer night's sky. My quivering lips could not exclaim; my prayer yielded up to The Greatest. The words a mere silent echo of formless praise...i succumb to silence.*

4. *The Majestic Greatness may claim my soul as a nocturnal cats prey...still, within i find no dismay. The primal sounds of their hunt above me are fitting to this eclectic escape.*

5. *In the cavern beneath the falls, meditating, praying, and not knowing if my wakening from slumber will find me unable to return to this body ever again.*

6. *See how, The Great Oneness brought forth this primeval beauty untouched by the abodes of men; The Greatness, The Creator, Whom is neither magnified nor reduced by the worship of this soul.*

7. *Yet, in the stillness an unspoken knowingness of kinship nurses my infant spirit. Oh, these thoughts, and unintelligible words within my breast cannot offer anything of worth to The Creator, The Maker of this Wondrous Perfect Order.*

8. *The chill wracking this body is stolen by sleep; eerily fears relinquish as i unfold in The Balance of the spinning giants sailing across galactic seas. Mortal time measured there, you and i -we can exist and be. The creatures to which this is their abode; submit one to the other in nature's harmony.*

9. *Out of place, alone here, before The Great Unknown Known, i await destiny.*

10. *Consciousness, steals me from my paradise. Great cats prowl above the caverns roof and though the might of their jaws would consume my mortality, they fear the gentle and powerful waters which chill and comfort me.*

11. *The One, Whom Orders The Perfect Balance veils me with angelic rushing waters. Guardians of this being that I am.*

12. *Forgotten are the fears that caused this mind to quake, and the colors of the rising star paint shadows on the towering cliffs.*

13. *The Greatest Creator of Balance, Who's Perfect Order's respite grants my body and soul this precious dawn; so still prostrate i fall.*

Of Wonder and Beauty

1. *In the deep universes of the oceans i have seen the most amazing forms of life; their evolution and conception far more than a chance happening of events. The colors, the shapes, the life within these creature and beings demands reverent pause...time stills.*

2. *Who is The One that Fashions this Splendid Beauty. Within the sublime random chaos of life the design becomes evident, revealed within the seas, the earth and skies, indeed...within me.*

3. *The One Designer of the Overwhelming Beauty presents The Reality of Existence and woe that i would reference this as GOD... in this heart it seems an offensive triviality.*

4. *i beg to The Forgiving One to heal me of such ignorant conceptions.*

5. *The One Who Subdues by the exponential powers of creation, all that is witnessed and unseen cannot be contained in the mind.*

6. *i only pray that these mere words might convey beyound reason this discovery of faith…this sojourn in belief.*

7. *The awesome wonders command me to the intuitive realms of knowing; a peaceful understanding within the heart; a realization that there is something far greater than our selves.*

8. *i pray humility will ever remain the garment of this soul.*

9. *i pray to The Forgiving, that this inferior voice be without arrogance; in this effort to acknowledge The Great Designer of Beauty with meager prose and inept artistry.*

10. *It is only an intended worship with no attempt to be measured worthy.*

11. *i beg that this subdued spirit embracing these days of abstention will honor The One Whom Subdues all things, knowing that The One Who Forgives and The One Who Fashions All Things is the keeper of souls.*

Pure Waters

1. *A child's tears flows from the river of Eden in the midst of heaven's garden. Where is this Eden they ask; and i said because you need to ask it will be challenging for you to find it. Feeling rebuked though i had spoken softly one among them said;*

2. *"You who are barely more than a pauper and one of such strange ways rebuke us with a child's riddle?"*

3. *i said to them; "Is it strange to feel the innocents sadness; is it really so odd to give up a meal so the child living in wretchedness hunger pangs may ease for a moment ... how can you deny others what you covet so much yourselves?"*

4. *And then they all left me to my mutterings and the ramblings of my pen. Save one, who came and sat beside me ... we have been*

traveling this poorly trodden path together ever since.

5. *Then the companion asked me how i found my way through the mire and often obscured road. i responded, "look there do you see them?"*

6. *i watched their quiet eyes follow my gaze and i watched as the power in them grew and the early morning colors were exchanged for the amber glows of the setting sun upon their countenance.*

7. *Yet, it seemed that only one moment had passed.*

8. *"Yes, there are the light of those few who passed this way before...their resonance remains for all who seek this way."*

9. *And then the young woman said; 'To Eden then."*

10. Thus we continue to journey…

Book of Thoughts

Volume III ~ **Divine Instance**

Forward

The old man said, "Do not think yourself mad." As he took a bony crooked finger and tapping my temple vigorously; "Go on tell your stories. It may be that one soul may be touched."

i turned to him miffed with his manners. It was then the familiarity of his countenance became clear for the first time. It only differed from mine with the etchings of time mapping seemingly hundreds of years upon his face.

He continued, "Intuition is intelligence from GOD, now see boy that you listen. You will travel farthest in your stillness, she will find you in your loneliness and you will love through your selflessness. So go boy and make it so."

Prologue

The myth and lore of the beginnings are testament to our innate reflection of realities beyond three dimensional spaces. This is The Unknown Known that so many seek to understand and others vehemently deny. As surely as the breath brings life to my mortal vessel; i bathe in the river of The Ever Living Infinite Reality and these stories unfold.

Sacred Breath

1. *This breath that fuels this life, our lives; its majesty and wonder; are too often lost in the panic and haste of our striving for the mundane.*

2. *The sacred breath, a sublime, invisible near weightless thing; the most precious generous gift from The Giving, Giver of All is The Trusted Power of our mortality.*

3. *Yet, with this breath we ignore the transcendent truth of The One Sustaining Provision; impressed with our own technical prowess.*

4. *In the glory of our breaths we can discover, engineer and invent; but yet we cannot create from the nothingness from which all things come.*

5. *We cannot fathom nothingness it is that which is incomprehensible to the intellect.*

6. *Too often our perceptions only exist in that in which we observe and measure.*

7. *All that we deem ours, cognition and intuition is a miraculous gift from The Sustaining Provision; only in this do we have dominion over other creatures of this earth.*

8. *The wonders of nature in the custody of our small fragile bodies; dynamic minds and too often vacant hearts.*

9. *Oh, that we would rekindle the wonder at the flight of the humming bird, the rising of the sun, the coo of a child, the golden sunlight filtering through leaves.*

10. *Yes, the soft countenance of the beloved in sleep; these are instances where The Divine is ever present.*

11. *How the overwhelmed heart is anxious to stand, bend, prostrate fall in submission to The Majestic Bountiful Creator of it All.*

Searching Heavens

1. *In the quiet of this room The One Who Opens all things, throws wide my heart to the pulse of the heavens and the song of this night.*

2. *Above the first heaven i watch the unending horizons of light, my mind melded into the expanse above the clouds. Nature's soft milky pyramids marked the skies above to the east as my spirit wings south.*

3. *Separating, abandoning the confines of physiology blue skies dissolve into the reaches of infinite space. This consciousness vaguely aware of me is imprinted with the wondrous and spectacular of The Supreme Knowing, The Omniscient One.*

4. *Recording words incapable of conveying The Knowledge of This Reality beyond form.*

5. The singing in my heart nor the dance of my spirit ceases as endless wonders unfold before a stilled mind and searching soul.

6. The senses that rule are sequestered in a chattering mind; the form that limited me falls away even in wakefulness. Only the ever emerging elegance assures that madness has not befallen me.

7. The One Who Constricts, and frames existence claims this consciousness. See how all things are refined within their nature, the governance of immutable laws.

8. Now, i am relieved of the burden and constriction of body and mind. Granted respite within the sublime spark hidden within the corporeal self. In this seclusion and abstention this heart opens by The Reliever who in this moment sweeps away the burden of mortality.

9. The dictates of culture, the clanging gongs of this mind abased my soul with the mundane

lessons of life. So, it is by the legacy of abstention, prayer, seclusion that this spirit now marries my soul, and The One Who Abases, grants respite.

10. *Seek the quietude within the Silence; within the quietude seek your heart. There within your heart is the true path to The Unknown Known ~ The Great, Majestic Sovereign Divine.*

11. *There is nothing in the conglomerate of electrostatic minutia of technology that can rival the light of your child's eyes.*

12. *Nor can distraction of media and sport triumph over the inadvertent soft smile your soul mate shines upon you.*

13. *That is truth that is reality.*

14. *Our breath is the sacred sublime; less we forget. We are not the makers or owners of*

the gentle wind within, the delicate force that powers all life. So, indeed it is a beautiful loan from The Great Unknown Known. It is a wondrous majesty that we share. If we can understand this, embrace it; how much more would we let kindness emanate from our beings.

15. They asked of me, "What is it that will keep us in the embrace of The Divine?" i repeated only what fell gently upon my ear. The angels' said,

16. Most precious in the lives of beloved are the little things we do, the silent thoughts of fondness unspoken and the quiet sweet things said that fill the heart so much they can no longer be held. These things are the binding jewels that shine light from the beloved's countenance when they are physically apart.

17. And i wondered at these whispers, and the angels continued,

18. *And when the beloved again embrace, iridescent rays are emitted to the heights of the heavens and we take up again in divine song.*

19. *Tears now stained my cheek and those too, of the ones who asked.*

20. *There is knowingness within the soul beyond the cognition of the mind; a reality intuited from the heart's consciousness, aligned with the resonance of The Divine. In such a moment there is truth, in such a moment this thing we call love can be found, gained and kept.*

21. *It is the balance of the Universal Presence known by many languages and names flowing through the blessing of our being. This balance of the Chi, Ki, Ruh, Life Force brings strength, health & serenity.*

The Arrival

1. *Maiden of the Fountain long have i waited your arrival. Upon the waters herein i first saw my reflection and any beauty in it eluded me accept fleeting moments.*

2. *My heart aching from its' parched spirit, my mind weary of its own folly; in this state of humility ... within the mirror of my soul i sense you.*

3. *A manifestation of an orphaned boy's angst is born of The Mercy of Divine Compassion. An apparition upon The Fountains waters where others came to visit and quench their thirst, but could not remain.*

4. *As they were on their own journey and were the teachers of my soul's suffering and flaws; the ones to clarify so that i could recognize you, the true, by The Grace of The Maker of Souls.*

5. *My melancholy heart's yearning unexplained teased my spirit and my body seemed severed from my unknown self.*

6. *Alone, I sipped the Fountains water never quenching the ache that pressed in the core of my mortality; just a measure that my cupped hands could hold; sustaining fleeting hope.*

7. *i lived within the solitude of entrapment of my own design; a shield from the world's harm but a fortress to my soul; yet keeping me from you.*

8. *You touch the well tended walls with courage and hope and the years of molded stone fortification crumbles like white ash; leaving me shaken wanting, knowing and unsure.*

9. *Now, with your arrival, my true self bathing in the radiant resonance of you; the*

fountain's reflective waters beauty and magnificence is far greater than i have ever known.

10. *The singing of our spirits ...the dance of brown bodies in this our sacred space ...our soul in humility lends its' voice to the chorus of angels. This ablution of the mind and heart is washed by the waters of our bodies and the rush of consecrated joy.*

11. *Desires of one another's' happiness is a pungent fragrance that envelopes these passions; an ardor that frees the minds egos and as brown bodies rhythms sincerely seep with joy.*

12. *Truly, a touch can be a prayer and the dance of glistening bodies syncopated meld to ebullient pleasure too, a gateway connecting our submission to The One... as the eagle on uncharted mountain peaks - our soul flies.*

13. *Truly this man, this woman with purifying hearts come together seeking the rapture within Divine Grace; and what the Supreme Maker of Hearts anoints let no person put asunder.*

14. *"That moment you put the music to all the words from this pen."*

15. *Say, Oh Divine All in All, My Compassionate Merciful Grace and Maker of Our Hearts, truly after hardship there is ease.*

16. *Holding fast to this rope of intent, many days and months will pass and the years mount all in this Divine Instance.*

17. *Amen.*

Epilogue

The journey is most often greater than the destination; for it is the steps that must be taken to become everything you are. One never stops becoming when touched with The Infinite.

Afterward

It is my deepest hope that these thoughts will be of benefit to others. At the very least inspire others introspection on the nature of who and what we really are. The flow of these words spring forth from a stream of consciousness that at times for me becomes overwhelming.

When i return to read and reflect on them, there is no sense of authorship in my mind. Again, i am most often swept away in a sea of reflections on how humanity is far more than just a collection of cells and biological systems. That esoteric and intangible thing we call consciousness, spirit, or soul, is a gateway of discovery to the vast and mysterious; Expansive Realties that can only be discovered through the intuitive super-consciousness of our minds and hearts.

It has been a blessing to have sat with saintly and brilliant sages who have seen, too, that which others can find useless or unnecessarily theosophical. So, in this i am thankful for the records of scriptures that open themselves to those whose intent, and indeed life's intention, is to understand what is unfathomable to the mind; but known in the soul.

The Kabala, The Torah, The Bible, The Vedas. The Upanishad and others provided a profound experience. Ultimately for me, The Qur'an gave credence and a pathway from which life's journey, pressed upon my heart with deepest meaning unfolding in a truth of pristine possibilities for living and refining ones character.

For in penetrating the veil of liturgy and legislation i found, as others before a magnanimous and wondrous teaching that softened my heart to relinquish much self; while being overwhelmed by a passion to serve. And to move beyond the restriction of humanness to the noblest of cause or at least the intentional struggle to do so. The Prophet (saws) of Islam taught that, 'The greatest jihad (struggle) is the jihad of nafs (the soul).'

This Unknown Known, the idea of GOD is a reality to me. And i would be remiss if i did not share the resonant words that have propelled me on this journey. They are known as the Asma'a ul' Husnah; often referred to as the 99 Attributes or Names of ALLAH.

They are for me three strands of thirty-three pearls laced within the Qur'an.

It is reported that Jesus said, 'Do not throw pearls to the swine.' They are the prayers, the remembrance and the mantra that launches the soul's rule over our ego; so that we can move beyond the human animal life to be the embodiment of the 'Divine Servant' in the world. As on far from such an attainment it is a precious and worthwhile endeavor.

'The best context of meaning in English of 'Asma'a ul' Husnah' can be said to mean, "The Beautiful Qualities and Attributes of the All and All." These qualities represent the character of, in Arabic simply, ALLAH.

Throughout this book you have surely noted specific and very unusual capitalizations within the verses. This is done in an effort to distinguish and reference these ninety-nine qualities or resonances in which the true Islamic teachings states are of ALLAH, but are reflected in the true believer, souls who seek the benefit and 'love for others as for themselves.'

When understood and by sharing truth and purity of intent these beautiful jewels can adorn the sincere person. Their power reflected in the believers living.

As the measuring of one's own ripple upon the pond of life becomes ever important to them; knowing that true submission to GOD is to serve humanity, safeguard the planet and to truly love others as we love ourselves.

It is then and only then, that we can best 'do unto others as we would unto ourselves.' And in the manner of true saints fulfill the Hippocratic Creed to 'Do no harm." We are all intended to by physicians of our soul.

"For each (person), there are angels in succession, before and behind him. They guard him by the Command of Allah. ALLAH does not change a people's condition, unless they change what is in their own hearts and soul." The Qur'an 13:11

The Attributes, vibrations, names of GOD as revealed in the Qur'an, that is the Asma'a ul' Hunah are included here in this Afterward to provide the reader with a greater understanding from which these thoughts manifest.

Arabic most often does not literally translate well into English. The etymological language bases of these two languages have no kinship. As the author of this small work, i have endeavored to give a contextual meaning, so that understanding of these to better embrace the mind and perhaps the heart. i pray that this is touched with clarity by the All Knowing. Truly in error in it is from me alone and forgiveness of the reader and The One asked in advance.

Paraphrasing the most famous Arabian Prophet, peace be upon him, 'if all the trees were pens and the oceans ink, it would not be enough to truly describe The Indescribable Source of All, ALLAH.'

These beautiful notes that sing from true souls are a glimpse of the unseen realities as revealed in the Qur'an and too often ignored by the Muslims of the world today. Their grace and beauty eluding the heart and not resonating in the character of our people; it is this failing that causes much of the strife of Muslims today and indeed within people of faith globally; thus manifesting a world in turmoil and sick with hatred, greed and war.

It is in sincere earnest that i pray this small effort may touch one heart as the noble teachings have touched mine.

It is said that the ninety-nine resonances of the Asma'a ul' Husnah are all contained within the single word ALLAH. Your consideration of these thoughts shared is appreciated. --- The Author

ALLAH, The Unique GOD, The One, ALL in ALL

ALLAH is the unique and exclusive name of GOD in Arabic used by Arabic speaking Christians and Muslims. This exclusive name contains all the ninety-nine attributes of GOD that can be embodied by mankind. Thus, allowing the believer to truly become GOD's reflection on earth, serving in life with the best interest of all foremost. This name contains countless more attributes that humanity cannot understand or embody. This name is resplendent and manifest with the resonance of the entirety of known and unknown universes.

The order of the 99 names, the attributes, the resonances lists from right to left, the same manner in which the Arabic language is written.

بِسْمِ اللهِ الرَّحْمٰنِ الرَّحِيمِ				
الرَّحْمٰن The Compassionate	الرَّحِيمُ The Most Merciful	الْمَلِكُ The Sovereign	الْقُدُّوسُ Free from Blemishes	السَّلَامُ The Giver of Peace
الْمُؤْمِنُ Giver of Peace	الْمُهَيْمِنُ Giver of Protection	الْعَزِيزُ The Mighty	الْجَبَّارُ Overpowering Lord	الْمُتَكَبِّرُ The Self Glorious
الْخَالِقُ The Creator	الْبَارِئُ The Giver of Life	الْمُصَوِّرُ Fashioner of shapes	الْغَفَّارُ Most Forgiving	الْقَهَّارُ Almighty Lord
الْوَهَّابُ Giver of all things	الرَّزَّاقُ The Sustainer	الْفَتَّاحُ Remover of Difficulties	الْعَلِيمُ The All Knowing	الْقَابِضُ The Straitener
الْبَاسِطُ Extender of Rizq	الْخَافِضُ One who Humbles	الرَّافِعُ The Exalter	الْمُعِزُّ Giver of Honour	الْمُذِلُّ Giver of Disgrace
السَّمِيعُ The All-Hearing	الْبَصِيرُ The All-Seeing	الْحَكَمُ The Judge	الْعَدْلُ The Just	اللَّطِيفُ Knower of Secrets
الْخَبِيرُ The Aware	الْحَلِيمُ The Clement	الْعَظِيمُ The Grand	الْغَفُورُ The All Forgiving	الشَّكُورُ The Grateful
الْعَلِيُّ The High	الْكَبِيرُ The Great	الْحَفِيظُ The Protector	الْمُقِيتُ Controller of things	الْحَسِيبُ The Reckoner
الْجَلِيلُ The Majestic	الْكَرِيمُ The Benevolent	الرَّقِيبُ The Caretaker	الْمُجِيبُ Responder to Du'aas	الْوَاسِعُ The Ample-Giving

الْحَقّ The True	الشَّهِيدُ The Omnipresent	الْبَاعِثُ The Resurrector	الْمَجِيدُ Most Venerable	الْوَدُودُ Most Loving	الْحَكِيمُ The Wise
الْمُحْصِي The One Who records	الْحَمِيدُ The Praiseworthy	الْوَلِيُّ The Patron	الْمَتِينُ The Firm	الْقَوِيُّ The Powerful	الْوَكِيلُ One in Charge
الْقَيُّومُ Self-Subsisting	الْحَيُّ Ever living	الْمُمِيتُ Giver of Death	الْمُحْيِي Giver of Life	الْمُعِيدُ One with power to Recreate	الْمُبْدِئُ The Originator
الْقَادِرُ The One with authority	الصَّمَدُ Free from Want	الْوَاحِدُالْأَحَدُ The One Unequalled		الْمَاجِدُ The Excellent	الْوَاجِدُ The Inventor
الظَّاهِرُ The Manifest	الْآخِرُ The Last	الْأَوَّلُ The First	الْمُؤَخِّرُ The One Who Retards	الْمُقَدِّمُ One Who causes Advancement	الْمُقْتَدِرُ The One with Full Authority
الْمُنْتَقِمُ The Taker of Retribution	التَّوَّابُ The Oft-returning	الْبَرُّ One who treats with Kindness	الْمُتَعَالِي Above the Creation	الْوَالِي The Authority	الْبَاطِنُ The Hidden
الْجَامِعُ The Assembler	الْمُقْسِطُ The Just	ذوالجلال والأكرام Possessor of Majesty and Benevolence	مَالِكُ الْمُلْكِ Possessor of Sovereignty	الرَّؤُوفُ The Affectionate	الْعَفُوُّ The Pardoner
النَّافِعُ The Benefactor	الضَّارُّ The Giver of Distress	الْمَانِعُ The Hinderer	الْمُعْطِي The Bestower	الْمُغْنِي The Enricher	الْغَنِيُّ Free from Want
الرَّشِيدُ Lover of Virtue	الْوَارِثُ The Supporter	الْبَاقِي The Eternal	الْبَدِيعُ The Deviser	الْهَادِي Giver of Guidance	النُّورُ The Light

الصَّبُورُ
Most Forbearing

Signings, Keynotes & Interviews with

*a'*Ali DeSousa

Contact: Martin Ide, 424-202-7714
Email: alandalustrust@gmail.com

Visit us on Facebook, login and go to:

https://www.facebook.com/aalidesousa
or
https://www.facebook.com/pages/aAlis-Angels/

Enjoy a'Ali's work on Canvas at:

http://fineartamerica.com/profiles/aalisa-desousa.html

Other Books by *a'*Ali DeSousa

Atlantic Crossing

This compelling story reads like a biopic film. One man's journey becomes a shared experience of the heart. The author's fluid use of language and ability to make a word worth a thousand pictures; justly earns the subtitle 'A Biopic in Print.'

a'Ali DeSousa renews our hope in humanity with this biographical tale of healing his own broken spirit from the turmoil of racial unrest in America by touching the sands of his maternal homeland and its people.

The authors' love for humanity, reminds us that our shared aspirations are what is important. He shows us that helping others is transformational.

Hearts Awaken

Compelling accounts from around the globe; through war, famine and more "HEARTS AWAKEN" ...where tragedy gives birth to triumph.